Visions of Wilderness

Visions of Wilderness

A Photographic Essay by Dewitt Jones

 Graphic Arts Center Publishing Co.
Portland, Oregon

Copyright © 1980 by Dewitt Jones
Graphic Arts Center Publishing Co.
P.O. Box 10306
Portland, Oregon 97210
503/224-7777

International Standard Book
Number: 0-912856-62-9
Library of Congress Catalog
Number: 80-65909

Designer: Jon Goodchild
Typesetting: Paul O. Giesey/
Adcrafters
Printing: Graphic Arts Center
Binding: Lincoln & Allen
Printed in the United States
of America

To Brian
my magical son

CONTENTS

I remember well a late Vermont winter afternoon when the sky had been mean and hostile since sunup, and in the west the last glimmer was doing its best to escape to a more hopeful place than New England. I heard a loud noise—could it be the mercury in the thermometer cracking the glass? My hearing is poor. It was Dewitt Jones stamping the snow from his feet on our porch. "I need to talk about photographing people out in the winter woods." He talked and talked, and finally there emerged the idea of joining the whiteness of snow to the whiteness of an infinity of white birches. At that point he jumped to his feet, saying: "I know a small mountain topped by a thousand birches; I'm off." By now it was impossibly dark and cold. I countered with a mug of rum and an open fire, but off he took himself. Early the next morning he admitted: "I almost didn't make it. The mountain was higher than I'd thought and the snow was to my waist most of the way. I floundered around a bit going up and coming down. Now I'm off to film a mother, father and their son skiing through those birches; it's going to be an amazing, wonderful world of whiteness." No Puritan girding up of loins to do duty there. It was all "damn the torpedoes; full steam ahead."

I have never seen Dewitt when his fires were not stoked by the joy of working. And for him the joy of working is the joy of seeing deeply. Like most men of talent, he contains a contradiction: he possesses tremendous energy and fire, yet he is able to slow down and look at things with attention—to quiet and allow the world to enter. As Flaubert wrote to de Maupassant: "To express what one wishes, one must look at things with enough attention to discover in them what has never been seen before."

What do I think of Dewitt's work? When I introduced one of his films to a Dartmouth College audience, I used some words adapted from Exodus: "Put off thy shoes from off thy feet, for the work you are about to see is holy ground." This may sound rather high flown, but I used these words not just because I think his work outstanding, but more because I think what he does is to save lives. Saving lives by making photographs? Am I exagerating? What do I mean?

I find each day's world more bewildering than the one before. The pages of the newspapers threaten a tomorrow even darker and colder. For the religious it must seem, as it did in biblical times, as if God had turned his face away from man. In this rapidly chilling world we must somewhere find warmth or die.

Where is warmth found? Certainly in the love of those close to us, but also in the love of life expressed by the creators: composers of music, writers, artists, photographers. With what they hand to us we can warm ourselves until this ice age of the spirit turns back to the sun again.

Dewitt's work is filled with enough beauty, light, and magic to warm us all. It is the perfect compliment to Eiseley, Dillard, Lopez and Jeffers. Together they are a vision that may indeed "save lives." Slow down, look deeply, you are in for a journey into wonders.

… I have tried to put down such miracles as can be evoked from common earth. But men see differently. I can at best report only from my own wilderness. The important thing is that each man possess such a wilderness and that he consider what marvels are to be observed there.

Loren Eiseley

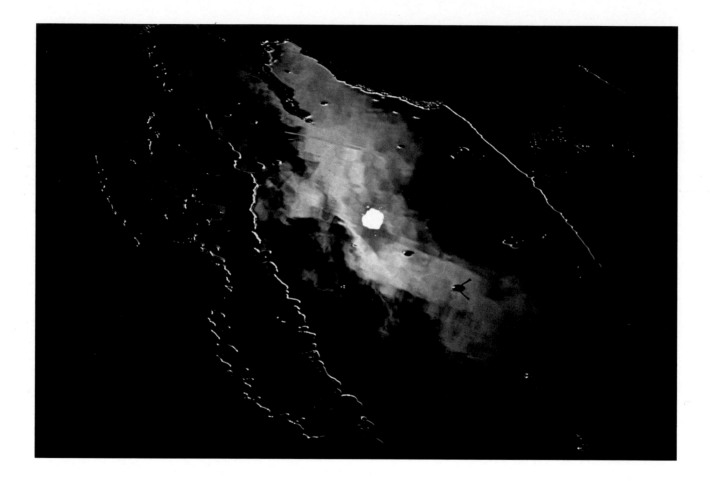

If there is magic on this planet,
it is contained in water.

Loren Eiseley

If there is magic on this planet, it is contained in water. Its least stir even, as now in a rain pond on a flat roof opposite my office, is enough to bring me searching to the window. A wind ripple may be translating itself into life. I have a constant feeling that some time I may witness that momentous miracle on a city roof, see life veritably and suddenly boiling out of a heap of rusted pipes and old television aerials. I marvel at how suddenly a water beetle has come and is submarining there in a spatter of green algae. Thin vapors, rust, wet tar and sun are an alembic remarkably like the mind; they throw off odorous shadows that threaten to take real shape when no one is looking.

Once in a lifetime, perhaps, one escapes the actual confines of the flesh. Once in a lifetime, if one is lucky, one so merges with sunlight and air and running water that whole eons, the eons that mountains and deserts know, might pass in a single afternoon without discomfort. The mind has sunk away into its beginnings among old roots and the obscure tricklings and movings that stir inanimate things. Like the charmed fairy circle into which a man once stepped, and upon emergence learned that a whole century had passed in a single night, one can never quite define this secret; but it has something to do, I am sure, with common water. Its substance reaches everywhere; it touches the past and prepares the future; it moves under the poles and wanders thinly in the heights of air. It can assume forms of exquisite perfection in a snowflake, or strip the living to a single shining bone cast up by the sea.

Many years ago, in the course of some scientific investigations in a remote western county, I experienced, by chance, precisely the sort of curious absorption by water—the extension of shape by osmosis—at which I have been hinting. You have probably never experienced in yourself the meandering roots of a whole watershed or felt your outstretched fingers touching, by some kind of clairvoyant extension, the

brooks of snow-line glaciers at the same time that you were flowing toward the Gulf over the eroded debris of worn-down mountains. A poet, MacKnight Black, has spoken of being "limbed . . . with waters gripping pole and pole." He had the idea, all right, and it is obvious that these sensations are not unique, but they are hard to come by; and the sort of extension of the senses that people will accept when they put their ear against a sea shell, they will smile at in the confessions of a bookish professor. What makes it worse is the fact that because of a traumatic experience in childhood, I am not a swimmer, and am inclined to be timid before any large body of water. Perhaps it was just this, in a way, that contributed to my experience.

As it leaves the Rockies and moves downward over the high plains towards the Missouri, the Platte River is a curious stream. In the spring floods, on occasion, it can be a mile-wide roaring torrent of destruction, gulping farms and bridges. Normally, however, it is a rambling, dispersed series of streamlets flowing erratically over great sand and gravel fans that are, in part, the remnants of a mightier Ice Age stream bed. Quicksands and shifting islands haunt its waters. Over it the prairie suns beat mercilessly throughout the summer. The Platte, "a mile wide and an inch deep," is a refuge for any heat-weary pilgrim along its shores. This is particularly true on the high plains before its long march by the cities begins.

The reason that I came upon it when I did, breaking through a willow thicket and stumbling out through ankle-deep water to a dune in the shade, is of no concern to this narrative. On various purposes of science I have ranged over a good bit of that country on foot, and I know the kinds of bones that come gurgling up through the gravel pumps, and the arrowheads of shining chalcedony that occasionally spill out of water-loosened sand. On that day, however, the sight of sky and willows and the weaving net of water murmuring a little in the shallows on its way to the Gulf stirred me, parched as I was with miles of walking, with a new idea: I was going to float. I was going to undergo a tremendous adventure.

The notion came to me, I suppose, by degrees. I had shed my clothes and was floundering pleasantly in a hole among some reeds when a great desire to stretch out and go with this gently insistent water began to pluck at me. Now to this bronzed, bold, modern generation, the struggle I waged with timidity while standing there in knee-deep water can only seem farcical; yet actually for me it was not so. A near-drowning accident in childhood had scarred my reactions; in addition to the fact that I was a nonswimmer, this "inch-deep river" was treacherous with holes and quicksands. Death was not precisely infrequent along its wandering and illusory channels. Like all broad wastes of this kind, where neither water nor land quite prevails, its thickets were lonely and untraversed. A man in trouble would cry out in vain.

I thought of all this, standing quietly in the water, feeling the sand shifting away under my toes. Then I lay back in the floating position that left my face to the sky, and shoved off. The sky wheeled over me. For an instant, as I bobbed into the main channel, I had the sensation of sliding down the vast tilted face of the continent. It was then that I felt the cold needles of the alpine springs at my fingertips, and the warmth of the Gulf pulling me southward. Moving with me, leaving its taste upon my mouth and spouting under me in dancing springs of sand, was the immense body of the continent itself, flowing like the river was flowing, grain by grain, mountain by mountain, down to the sea. I was streaming over ancient sea beds thrust aloft where giant reptiles had once sported; I was wearing down the face of time and trundling cloud-wreathed ranges into oblivion. I touched my margins with the delicacy of a crayfish's antennae, and felt great fishes glide about their work.

I drifted by stranded timber cut by beaver in mountain fastnesses; I slid over shallows that had buried the broken axles of prairie schooners and the mired bones of mammoth. I was streaming alive through the hot and working ferment of the sun, or oozing secretively through shady thickets. I *was* water and the unspeakable alchemies that gestate and take shape in water, the slimy jellies that under the enormous magnification of the sun writhe and whip upward as great barbeled fish mouths, or sink indistinctly back into the murk out of which they arose. Turtle and fish and the pinpoint chirpings of individual frogs are all watery projections, concentrations—as man himself is a concentration—of that indescribable and liquid brew which is compounded in varying proportions of salt and sun and time. It has appearances, but at its heart lies water, and as I was finally edged gently against a sand bar and dropped like any log, I tottered as I rose. I knew once more the body's revolt against emergence into the harsh and unsupporting air, its reluctance to break contact with that mother element which still, at this late point in time, shelters and brings into being nine tenths of everything alive.

As for men, those myriad little detached ponds with their own swarming corpuscular life, what were they but a way that water has of going about beyond the reach of rivers? I, too, was a microcosm of pouring rivulets and floating driftwood gnawed by the mysterious animacules of my own creation. I was three fourths water, rising and subsiding according to the hollow knocking in my veins: a minute pulse like the eternal pulse that lifts Himalayas and which, in the following systole, will carry them away.

Thoreau, peering at the emerald pickerel in Walden Pond, called them "animalized water" in one of his moments of strange insight. If he had been possessed of the geological knowledge so laboriously accumulated since his time, he might have gone further and amusedly detected in the planetary rumblings and eructations which so delighted him in the gross habits of certain frogs, signs of that dark interior stress which has reared sea bottoms up to mountainous heights. He might have developed an acute inner ear for the sound of the surf on Cretaceous beaches where now the wheat of Kansas rolls. In any case, he would have seen, as the long trail of life was unfolded by the fossil hunters, that his animalized water had changed its shapes eon by eon to the beating of the earth's dark millennial heart. In the swamps of the low continents, the amphibians had flourished and had their day; and as the long skyward swing—the isostatic response of the crust—had come about, the era of the cooling grasslands and mammalian life had come into being.

A few winters ago, clothed heavily against the weather, I wandered several miles along one of the tributaries of that same Platte I had floated down years before. The land was stark and ice-locked. The rivulets were frozen, and over the marshlands the willow thickets made such an array of vertical lines against the snow that tramping through them produced strange optical illusions and dizziness. On the edge of a frozen backwater, I stopped and rubbed my eyes. At my feet a raw prairie wind had swept the ice clean of snow. A peculiar green object caught my eye; there was no mistaking it.

Staring up at me with all his barbels spread pathetically, frozen solidly in the wind-ruffled ice, was a huge familiar face. It was one of those catfish of the twisting channels, those dwellers in the yellow murk, who had been about me and beneath me on the day of my great voyage. Whatever sunny dream had kept him paddling there while the mercury plummeted downward and that Cheshire smile froze slowly, it would be hard to say. Or perhaps he was trapped in a blocked channel and had simply kept swimming until the ice contracted around him. At any rate, there he would lie till the spring thaw.

At that moment I started to turn away, but something in the bleak, whiskered face reproached me, or perhaps it was the river calling to her children. I termed it science, however—a convenient rational phrase I reserve for such occasions—and decided that I would cut the fish out of the ice and take him home. I had no intention of eating him. I was merely struck by a sudden impulse to test the survival qualities of high-plains fishes, particularly fishes of this type who get themselves immured in oxygenless ponds or in cut-off oxbows buried in winter drifts. I blocked him out as gently as possible and dropped him, ice and all, into a collecting can in the car. Then we set out for home.

Unfortunately, the first stages of what was to prove a remarkable resurrection escaped me. Cold and tired after a long drive, I deposited the can with its melting water and ice in the basement. The accompanying corpse I anticipated I would either dispose of or dissect on the following day. A hurried glance had revealed no signs of life.

To my astonishment, however, upon descending into the basement several hours later, I heard stirrings in the receptacle and peered in. The ice had melted. A vast pouting mouth ringed with sensitive feelers confronted me, and the creatures gills labored slowly. A thin stream of silver bubbles rose to the surface and popped. A fishy eye gazed up at me protestingly.

"A tank," it said. This was no Walden pickerel. This was a yellow-green, mud-grubbing, evil-tempered inhabitant of floods and droughts and cyclones. It was the selective product of the high continent and the waters that pour across it. It had outlasted prairie blizzards that left cattle standing frozen upright in the drifts.

"I'll get the tank," I said respectfully.

He lived with me all that winter, and his departure was totally in keeping with his sturdy, independent character. In the spring a migratory impulse or perhaps sheer boredom struck him. Maybe, in some little lost corner of his brain, he felt, far off, the pouring of the mountain waters through the sandy coverts of the Platte. Anyhow, something called to him, and he went. One night when no one was about, he simply jumped out of his tank. I found him dead on the floor next morning. He had made his gamble like a man—or, I should say, a fish. In the proper place it would not have been a fool's gamble. Fishes in the drying shallows of intermittent prairie streams who feel their confinement and have the impulse to leap while there is yet time may regain the main channel and survive. A million ancestral years had gone into that jump, I thought as I looked at him, a million years of climbing through prairie sunflowers and twining in and out through the pillared legs of drinking mammoth.

"Some of your close relatives have been experimenting with air breathing," I remarked, apropos of nothing, as I gathered him up. "Suppose we meet again up there in the cottonwoods in a million years or so."

I missed him a little as I said it. He had for me the kind of lost archaic glory that comes from the water brotherhood. We were both projections out of that timeless ferment and locked as well in some greater unity that lay incalculably beyond us. In many a fin and reptile foot I have seen myself passing by—some part of myself, that is, some part that lies unrealized in the momentary shape I inhabit. People have occasionally written me harsh letters and castigated me for a lack of faith in man when I have ventured to speak of this matter in print. They distrust, it would seem, all shapes and thoughts but their own. They would bring God into the compass of a shopkeeper's understanding and confine Him to those limits, lest He proceed to some unimaginable and shocking act—create perhaps, as a casual afterthought, a being more beautiful than man. As for me, I believe nature capable of this, and having been part of the flow of the river, I feel no envy—any more than the frog envies the reptile or an ancestral ape should envy man.

Every spring in the wet meadows and ditches I hear a little shrilling chorus which sounds for all the world like an endlessly reiterated "We're here, we're here, we're here." And so they are, as frogs, of course. Confident little fellows. I suspect that to some greater ear than ours, man's optimistic pronouncements about his role and destiny may make a similar little ringing sound that travels a small way out into the night. It is only its nearness that is offensive. From the heights of a mountain, or a marsh at evening, it blends, not too badly, with all the other sleepy voices that, in croaks or chirrups, are saying the same thing.

After a while the skilled listener can distinguish man's noise from the katydid's rhythmic assertion, allow for the offbeat of a rabbit's thumping, pick up the autumnal monotone of crickets, and find in all of them a grave pleasure without admitting any to a place of preëminence in his thoughts. It is when all these voices cease and the waters are still, when along the frozen river nothing cries, screams or howls, that the enormous mindlessness of space settles down upon the soul. Somewhere out in that waste of crushed ice and reflected stars, the black waters may be running, but they appear to be running without life toward a destiny in which the whole of space may be locked in some silvery winter of dispersed radiation.

It is then, when the wind comes straitly across the barren marshes and the snow rises and beats in endless waves against the traveler, that I remember best, by some trick of the imagination, my summer voyage on the river. I remember my green extensions, my catfish nuzzlings and minnow wrigglings, my gelatinous materializations out of the mother ooze. And as I walk on through the white smother, it is the magic of water that leaves me a final sign.

Men talk much of matter and energy, of the struggle for existence that molds the shape of life. These things exist, it is true; but more delicate, elusive, quicker than the fins in water, is that mysterious principle known as "organization," which leaves all other mysteries concerned with life stale and insignificant by comparison. For that without organization life does not persist is obvious. Yet this organization itself is not strictly the product of life, nor of selection. Like some dark and passing shadow within matter, it cups out the eyes' small windows or spaces the notes of a meadow lark's song in the interior of a mottled egg. That principle—I am beginning to suspect—was there before the living in the deeps of water.

The temperature has risen. The little stinging needles have given way to huge flakes floating in like white leaves blown from some great tree in open space. In the car, switching on the lights, I examine one intricate crystal on my sleeve before it melts. No utilitarian philosophy explains a snow crystal, no doctrine of use or disuse. Water has merely leapt out of vapor and thin nothingness in the night sky to array itself in form. There is no logical reason for the existence of a snowflake any more than there is for evolution. It is an apparition from that mysterious shadow world beyond nature, that final world which contains—if anything contains—the explanation of men and catfish and green leaves.

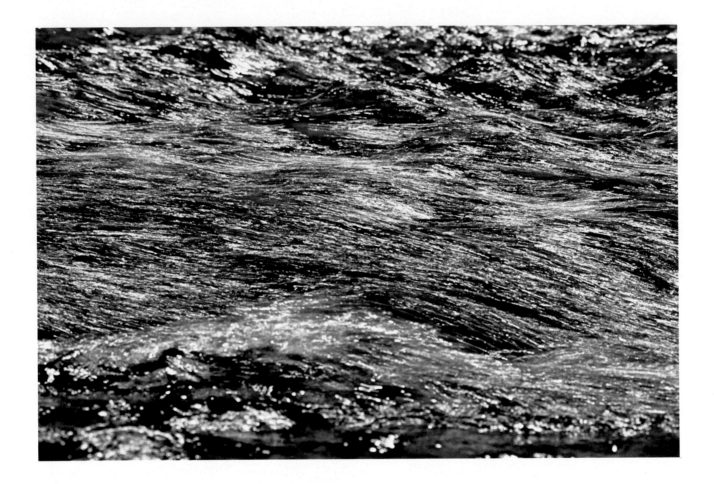

I was three fourths water,
rising and subsiding according to the hollow knocking in my veins:
a minute pulse like the eternal pulse
that lifts Himalayas and which, in the following systole,
will carry them away.

Loren Eiseley

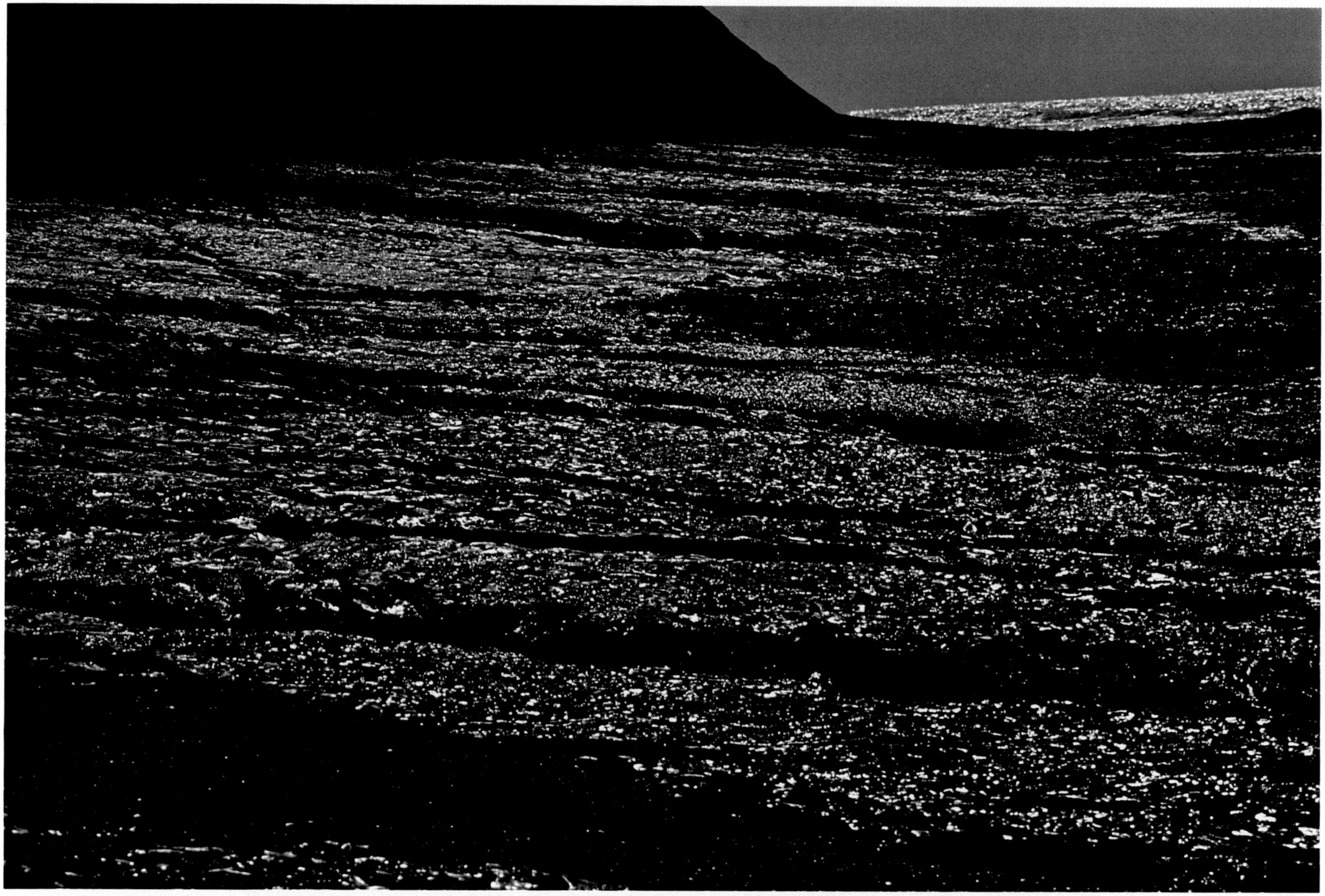

*There is no logical reason for the existence of a snowflake
any more than there is for evolution. It is an apparition
from that mysterious shadow world beyond nature,
that final world which contains —if anything contains —
the explanation of men and catfish and green leaves.*

Loren Eiseley

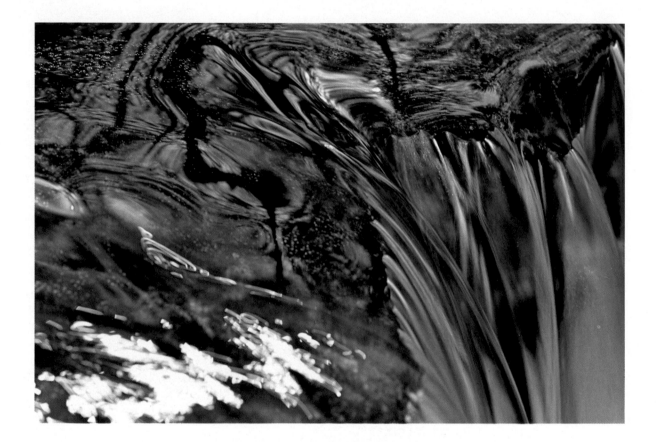

We were both projections out of that timeless ferment
and locked as well in some greater unity
that lay incalculably beyond....

Loren Eiseley

*There was only silence....There were no cells moving,
and yet there were cells. I could see the shape
of the land, how it lay holding silence. Its poise and its
stillness were unendurable, like the ring of the silence
you hear in your skull when you're little and notice
you're living....*

Annie Dillard

There is a place called "the farm" where I lived once, in a time that was very lonely. Fortunately I was unconscious of my loneliness then, and felt it only deeply, bewildered, in the half-bright way that a puppy feels pain.

I loved the place, and still do. It was an ordinary farm, a calf-raising, haymaking farm, and very beautiful. Its flat, messy pastures ran along one side of the central portion of a quarter-mile road in the central part of an island, an island in Puget Sound, so that from the high end of the road you could look west toward the Pacific, to the Sound and its hundred islands, and from the other end—and from the farm—you could see east to the water between you and the mainland, and beyond it the mainland's mountains slicked smooth with snow.

I liked the clutter about the place, the way everything blossomed or seeded or rusted; I liked the hundred half-finished projects, the smells, and the way the animals always broke loose. It is calming to herd animals. Often a regular rodeo breaks out— two people and a clever cow can kill a morning—but still, it is calming. You laugh for a while, exhausted, and silence is restored; the beasts are back in their pastures, the fences not fixed but disguised as if they were fixed, ensuring the animals' temporary resignation; and a great calm descends, a lack of urgency, a sense of having to invent something to do until the next time you must run and chase cattle.

The farm seemed eternal in the crude way the earth does—extending, that is, a very long time. The farm was as old as earth, always there, as old as the island, the Platonic form of "farm," of human society itself and at large, a piece of land eaten and replenished a billion summers, a piece of land worked on, lived on, grown over, plowed under, and stitched again and again, with fingers or with leaves, in and out and into human life's thin weave. I lived there once.

I lived there once and I have seen, from behind the barn, the long roadside pastures heaped with silence. Behind the rooster, suddenly, I saw the silence heaped on the fields like trays. That day the green hayfields supported silence evenly sown; the fields bent just so under the even pressure of silence, bearing it, even, palming it aloft: cleared fields, part of a land, a planet, that did not buckle beneath the heel of silence, nor split up scattered to bits, but instead lay secret, disguised as time and matter as though that were nothing, ordinary—disguised as fields like those which bear the silence only because they are spread, and the silence spreads over them, great in size.

I do not want, I think, ever to see such a sight again. That there is loneliness here I had granted, in the abstract—but not, I thought, inside the light of God's presence, inside his sanction, and signed by his name.

I lived alone in the farmhouse and rented; the owners, Angus and Lynn, in their twenties, lived in another building just over the yard. I had been reading and restless for two or three days. It was morning. I had just read at breakfast an Updike story, "Packed Dirt, Churchgoing, A Dying Cat, A Traded Car," which moved me. I heard our own farmyard rooster and two or three roosters across the street screeching. I quit the house, hoping at heart to see Lynn or Angus, but immediately to watch our rooster as he crowed.

It was Saturday morning late in the summer, in early September, clear-aired and still. I climbed the barnyard fence between the poultry and the pastures; I watched the red rooster, and the rooster, reptilian, kept one alert and alien eye on me. He pulled his extravagant neck to its maximum length, hauled himself high on his legs, stretched his beak as if he were gagging, screamed, and blinked. It was a ruckus. The din came from everywhere, and only the most rigorous application of reason could persuade me that it proceeded in its entirety from this lone and maniac bird.

After a pause, the roosters across the street would start, answering the proclamation, or cranking out another round, arrhythmically, interrupting. In the same way there is no pattern nor sense to the massed stridulations of cicadas; their skipped beats, enjambments, and failed alterations jangle your spirits, as though each of those thousand insects, each with identical feelings, were stubbornly deaf to the others, and loudly alone.

I shifted along the fence to see if Lynn or Angus was coming or going. To the rooster I said nothing, but only stared. And he stared at me; we were both careful to keep the wooden fence slat from our line of sight, so that his profiled eye and my two eyes could meet. From time to time I looked beyond the pastures to learn if anyone might be seen on the road.

When I was turned away in this manner, the silence gathered and struck me. It bashed me broadside from nowhere, as if I'd been hit by a plank. It dropped from the heavens above me like yard goods; ten acres of fallen, invisible sky choked the fields. The pastures on either side of the road turned green in a surrealistic fashion, monstrous, impeccable, as if they were holding their breath. The roosters stopped. All the things of the world—the fields and the fencing, the road, a parked orange truck— were stricken and self-conscious. A world pressed down on their surfaces, a world battered just within their surfaces, and that real world, so near to emerging, had got stuck.

There was only silence. It was the silence of matter caught in the act and embarrassed. There were no cells moving, and yet there were cells. I could see the shape of the land, how it lay holding silence. Its poise and its stillness were unendurable, like the ring of the silence you hear in your skull when you're little and notice you're living, the ring which resumes later in life when you're sick.

There were flies buzzing over the dirt by the henhouse, moving in circles and buzzing, black dreams in chips off the one long dream, the dream of the regular world. But the silent fields were the real world, eternity's outpost in time, whose look I remembered but never like this, this God-blasted, paralyzed day. I felt myself tall and vertical, in a blue shirt, self-conscious, and wishing to die. I heard the flies again; I looked at the rooster who was frozen looking at me.

Then at last I heard whistling, human whistling far on the air, and I was not able to bear it. I looked around, heartbroken; only at the big yellow Charolais farm far up the road was there motion—a woman, I think, dressed in pink, and pushing a wheelbarrow easily over the grass. It must have been she who was whistling and heaping on top of the silence those hollow notes of song. But the slow sound of the music—the beautiful sound of the music ringing the air like a stone bell—was isolate and detached. The notes spread into the general air and became the weightier part of silence, silence's last straw. The distant woman and her wheelbarrow were flat and detached, like mechanized and pink-painted properties for a stage. I stood in pieces, afraid I was unable to move. Something had unhinged the world. The houses and roadsides and pastures were buckling under the silence. Then a Labrador, black, loped up the distant driveway, fluid and cartoonlike, toward the pink woman. I had to try to turn away. Holiness is a force, and like the others can be resisted. It was given, but I didn't want to see it, God or no God. It was as if God had said, "I am here, but not as you have known me. This is the look of silence, and of loneliness unendurable: it too has always been mine, and now will be yours." I was not ready for a life of sorrow, sorrow deriving from knowledge I could just as well stop at the gate.

I turned away, willful, and the whole show vanished. The realness of things disassembled. The whistling became ordinary, familiar; the air above the fields released its pressure and the fields lay hooded as before. I myself could act. Looking to the rooster I whistled to him myself, softly, and some hens appeared at the chicken house window, greeted the day, and fluttered down.

Several months later, walking past the farm on the way to a volleyball game, I remarked to a friend, by way of information, "There are angels in those fields." Angels! That silence so grave and so stricken, that choked and unbearable green! I have rarely been so surprised at something I've said. Angels! What are angels? I had never thought of angels, in any way at all.

From that time I began to think of angels. I considered that sights such as I had seen of the silence must have been shared by the people who said they saw angels. I began to review the thing I had seen that morning. My impression now of those fields is of thousands of spirits—spirits trapped, perhaps, by my refusal to call them more fully, or by the paralysis of my own spirit at that time—thousands of spirits, angels in fact, almost discernible to the eye, and whirling. If pressed I would say they were three or four feet from the ground. Only their motion was clear (clockwise, if you insist); that, and their beauty unspeakable.

There are angels in those fields, and, I presume, in all fields, and everywhere else. I would go to the lions for this conviction, to witness this fact. What all this means about perception, or language, or angels, or my own sanity, I have no idea.

There are angels in those fields,
and, I presume, in all fields,
and everywhere else.

Annie Dillard

I awoke one night and thought I heard rain—it was the dry needles of fir trees falling on the roof. Men with an intolerable air of condolence have appeared, as though drawn by the smell of death, dressed comfortably, speaking a manipulated tongue, terminally evil. They have inquired into the purchase of our homes. And reporters come and go, outraged over the absence of brown trout, which have never been here. The river like some great whale lies dying in the forest.

In the years we have been here I have trained myself to listen to the river, not in the belief that I could understand what it said, but only from one day to the next know its fate. The river's language arose principally from two facts: the slightest change in its depth brought it into contact with a different portion of the stones along its edges and the rocks and boulders mid-stream that lay in its way, and so changed its tone; and although its movement around one object may seem uniform at any one time it is in fact changeable. Added to these major variations are the landings of innumerable insects on its surface, the breaking of its waters by fish, the falling into it of leaves and twigs, the slooshing of raccoons, the footfalls of deer; ultimately these are the only commentary on the river's endless reading of the surface of the earth over which it flows.

It was in this way that I learned before anyone else of the coming drought. Day after day as the river fell by imperceptible increments its song changed, notes came that were unknown to me. I mentioned this to no one, but each morning when I awoke I went immediately to the river's edge and listened. It was as though I could hear the sound rain begins to make in a country where it is not going to come for a long time.

As the water fell, however, nothing unexpected was uncovered, although the effect of standing in areas once buried beneath the roar of the river's current was unsettling. I found only one made object, a wheel, the kind you find on the back of a child's tricycle. But I didn't look as closely as the others. The wailing of the river over its last stones was difficult to bear, yet it was this that drew me back each day, as one visits those dying hopelessly in a hospital room. During those few hours each morning I would catch stranded fish barehanded in shallow pools and release them where the river still flowed. The bleaching of algae once waving green underwater to white; river stones once cool now hot to the touch and dry; spider webs stretched where there had been salmon eggs; snakes where there had been trout—it was though the river had been abandoned.

During those summer days, absorbed with the death of the river and irritated at the irreverent humor of weather forecasters in distant cities, I retreated into a state of isolation. I fasted and abstained as much as I felt appropriate from water. These were only gestures, of course, but even as a boy I knew a gesture might mean life or death and I believed the universe was similarly triggered.

From this point on, the song that came out of the river did not bother me as much. I sat out of the way of the pounding sun, in dark rocks shaded by the overhanging branches of alders along the bank. Their dry leaves, stirred by the breeze, fell brittle and pale around me. I slept on the bank regularly now. I would say very simple prayers in the evening, only an expression of camaraderie, stretching my fingers gently into the darkness toward the inchoate source of the river's strangulation. I did not beg. There was a power to dying, and it should be done with grace. I was only making a gesture on the shore, a speck in the steep, brutal dryness of the valley by a dying river.

In moments of great depression, of an unfathomable compassion in myself, I would make the agonized and tentative movements of a dance, like a long-legged bird. I would exhort the river.

What death we saw. Garter snake stiff as a twig in the rocks. Trees (young ones, too young) crying out in the night, shuddering, dropping all their leaves. Farther from the river, birds falling dead in thickets, animals dead on the paths, their hands stiffened in gestures of bewilderment and beseeching;

the color gone out of the eyes of any creature you met, for whom, out of respect, you would step off the path to allow to pass.

Where a trickle of water still flowed there was an atmosphere of truce, more dangerous than one might imagine. As deer and coyote sipped from the same tiny pool they abrogated their agreement, and the deer contemplated the loss of the coyote as he would the loss of a friend; for the enemy, like the friend, made you strong. I was alert for such moments, for they were augury, but I was as wary of them as of any lesson learned in death.

One moonlit evening I dreamed of a certain fish. The fish was gray-green against light-colored stones at the bottom of a deep pool, breathing a slow, unperturbed breathing, the largest fish I had ever imagined living in the river. The sparkling of the water around him and the sound of it cascading over the creek bed made me weak and I awoke suddenly, convulsed. I knew the fish. I knew the place. I set out immediately.

The dry riverbed was only a clatter of teetering stones now, ricocheting off my feet as I passed, bone weary, feeling disarmed by hunger, by the dimness of the night, and by the irrefutable wisdom and utter foolishness of what I was doing. As I drew near the mouth of the creek the fish began to loom larger and larger and I could feel—as though my hands were extended to a piece of cloth flapping in the darkness—both the hope and the futility of such acts.

I found the spot where the creek came in and went up it. I had seen the fish once in a deep pool below a rapids where he had fed himself too well and grown too large to escape. There was a flow of night air coming down the creek bed, rattling dry leaves. In the faint moonlight a thousand harlequin beetles suddenly settled on my clothing and I knew how close I was to a loss of conviction, to rage, to hurling what beliefs I had like a handful of pebbles into the bushes.

The beetles clung to the cloth, moved through my hair, came into the cups of my hands as I walked, and as suddenly were gone, and the area I stood in was familiar, the fish before me. The rapids were gone. The pool had become a pit. In its lowest depression the huge fish lay motionless, but for the faint lifting of a gill cover. I climbed down to him and wrapped him in my shirt, soaked in the pool. I had expected, I think, a fight, to be punched in that pit by the fish who lay in my arms now like a cold lung.

Climbing out of there, stopping wherever I could to put his head under in some miserable pool, hurrying, I came to the river and the last trickle of water, where I released him without ceremony.

I knew, as I had known in the dream, the danger I was in but I knew, too, that without such an act of self-assertion no act of humility had meaning.

By now the river was only a whisper. I stood at the indistinct edge and exhorted what lay beyond the river, which now seemed more real than the river itself. With no more strength than there is in a bundle of sticks I tried to dance, to dance the dance of the long-legged birds who lived in the shallows. I danced it because I could not think of anything more beautiful.

The turning came during the first days of winter. Lynx came down from the north to what was left of the river. Deer were with him. And from some other direction Racoon and Porcupine. And from downriver Weasel and White-footed Mouse, and from above Blue Heron and Goshawk. Badger came up out of the ground with Mole. They stood near me in staring silence and I was afraid to move. Finally Blue Heron spoke: "We were the first people here. We gave away all the ways of living. Now no one remembers how to live anymore, so the river is drying up. Before we could ask for rain there had to be someone to do something completely selfless, with no hope of success. You went after that fish, and then at the end you were trying to dance. A person cannot be afraid of being foolish. For everything, every gesture, is sacred.

"Now, stand up and learn this dance. It is going to rain."

We danced together on the bank. And the songs we danced to were the river songs I remembered from long ago. We danced until I could not understand the words but only the sounds, and the sounds were unmistakably the sound rain makes when it is getting ready to come into a country.

I awoke in harsh light one morning, moved back into the trees and fell asleep again. I awoke later to what I thought were fir needles falling on my cheeks but these were drops of rain.

It rained for weeks. Not hard, but steadily. The river came back easily. There were no floods. People said it was a blessing. They offered explanations enough. Backs were clapped, reputations lost and made, the seeds of future argument and betrayal sown, wounds suffered and allowed, pride displayed. It was no different from any other birth but for lack of joy and, for that, stranger than anything you can imagine, inhuman and presumptuous. But people go their way, and with reason; and the hardness for some is all but unfathomable, and so begs forgiveness. Everyone has to learn how to die, that song, that dance, alone and in time.

The river has come back to fit between its banks. To stick your hands into the river is to feel the cords that bind the earth together in one piece. The sound of it at a distance is like wild horses in a canyon, going sure-footed away from the smell of a cougar come to them faintly on the wind.

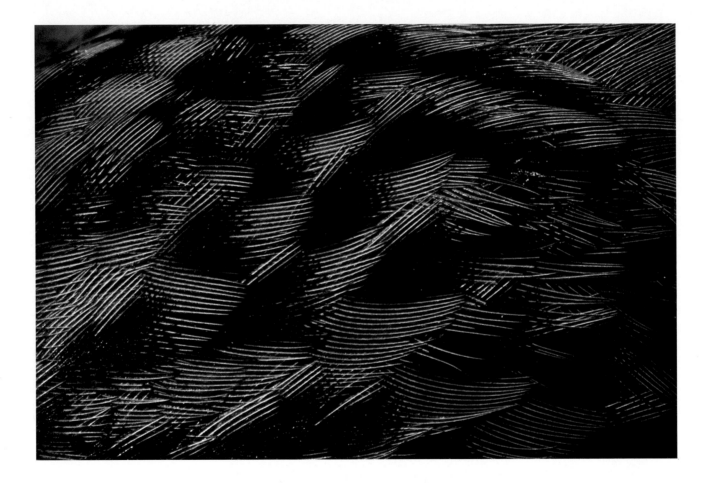

We danced together on the bank.
And the songs we danced were the songs
I remember from long ago.
We danced until I could not understand the words
but only the sounds....

Barry Lopez

Mountains, a moment's earth-waves rising and hollowing; the
     earth too's an ephemerid; the stars—
Short-lived as grass the stars quicken in the nebula and dry in their
     summer, they spiral
Blind up space, scattered black seeds of a future; nothing lives
     long, the whole sky's
Recurrences tick the seconds of the hours of the ages of the gulf
     before birth, and the gulf
After death is like dated: to labor eighty years in a notch of
     eternity is nothing too tiresome,
Enormous repose after, enormous repose before, the flash of
     activity.
Surely you never have dreamed the incredible depths were pro-
     logue and epilogue merely
To the surface play in the sun, the instant of life, what is called
     life? I fancy
That silence is the thing, this noise a found word for it; inter-
     jection, a jump of the breath at that silence;
Stars burn, grass grows, men breathe: as a man finding treasure
     says "Ah!" but the treasure's the essence;
Before the man spoke it was there, and after he has spoken he
     gathers it, inexhaustible treasure.

ABOUT THE ARTISTS

Dewitt Jones has been a photographer and filmmaker for the past fourteen years. His books include JOHN MUIR'S AMERICA, WHAT THE ROAD PASSES BY, and ROBERT FROST: A TRIBUTE TO THE SOURCE. His photographic essays appear regularly in the *National Geographic* magazine, and his films have twice been nominated for Academy Awards. He lives in Bolinas, California with his wife, Babs, and his son, Brian.

Loren Eiseley, was an author of many award winning books, and is well remembered both as a naturalist and as a humanist. His work is represented in many anthologies of English prose. In 1971 he was elected to the National Institute of Arts and Letters.

Annie Dillard is a poet and essayist now living in the Pacific Northwest. Her book, PILGRIM AT TINKER CREEK, won a Pulitzer Prize in 1974.

Barry Lopez is a contributing editor to *Harper's* and *North American Review*. He has authored several books including OF WOLVES AND MEN and DESERT NOTES: REFLECTIONS IN THE EYE OF A RAVEN. He lives near Finn Rock, Oregon.

Robinson Jeffers was a poet and playwright who made his home in Carmel, California. He won a Pulitzer Prize in 1954 and was a member of the National Institute of Arts and Letters.

ABOUT THE PHOTOGRAPHS

All of the photographs in this book were taken with Nikkormat 35mm SLR camera bodies and Nikkor lenses.

Cover. Nicasio reservoir, Nicasio, Ca.
20mm f/4 lens, K 25.

2. Kluane National Park, Yukon, Canada.
20mm F/3.5 lens, K 25.

6. Gustavus, Alaska.
20mm f/3.5 lens, K 25.

8. Sonora, Ca.
80-200mm f/4.5 zoom lens, K 25.

13. Bolinas, Ca.
20mm f/4 lens, K 25.

14. Nicasio reservoir, Nicasio, Ca.
55mm f/3.5 Micro lens, K 25.

15. Bolinas, Ca.
80-200mm f/4.5 zoom lens, K 64.

16. Sun reflection, Thetford, Vt.
55mm f/3.5 Micro lens, K 25.

17. Yosemite National Park, Ca.
80-200mm f/4.5 zoom lens, K 25.

19. Bolinas Lagoon, Bolinas, Ca.
20mm f/4 lens, K 25.

20. Stinson Beach, Ca.
500mm f/5 Mirror lens, K 64.

25. Nemo Creek near New Denver, British Columbia.
200mm f/4 lens, K II.

26. Tuolumne River, Yosemite National Park, Ca.
80-200mm f/4.5 zoom lens, K 25.

27. Agate Beach, Bolinas, Ca.
80-200mm f/4.5 zoom lens, K 25.

28. Cloud, New Denver, British Columbia.
105mm f/3.5 lens, K II.

29. Ice on Mulvey Lake, Valhalla Range, British Columbia.
80-200mm f/4.5 zoom lens, K 25.

31. Looking down on Slocan Lake, British Columbia during a snow storm.
20mm f/4 lens, K 25.

32. Yosemite National Park, Ca.
20mm f/4 lens, K 64.

33. Silversword plant, Haleakala Crater, Maui, Hawaii.
20mm f/4 lens, K 25.

34. Fern Spring, Yosemite National Park, Ca.
55mm f/3.5 Micro lens, K II.

35. New Denver, British Columbia
200mm f/4 lens, K II.

36. Spring forest, Sherborn, Mass.
200mm f/4 lens, K II.

37. Yosemite National Park, Ca.
200mm f/4 lens, K 25.

38. Maple tree, Santa Rosa, Ca.
80-200mm f/4.5 zoom lens, K 25.

39. Merced River, Yosemite National
    Park, Ca.
    80-200mm f/4.5 zoom lens, K 25.

41. Crane Flat, Yosemite National Park, Ca.
    28mm f/3.5 lens, K II.

48. Slocan, British Columbia.
    28mm f/3.5 lens, K II.

49. Bolinas, Ca.
    105mm f/3.5 lens, K 25.

50. Redbud, El Portal, Ca.
    20mm f/4 lens, K 25.

51. Livermore, Ca.
    80-200mm f/4.5 zoom lens, K 25.

53. Windy Hill, Portola Valley, Ca.
    20mm f/4 lens, K 25.

54. Coastal Redwoods, Klamath, Ca.
    20mm f/4 lens, K 25.

55. Heather farm, Muir Beach, Ca.
    80-200mm f/4.5 zoom lens, EPD 200

57. Haleakala Crater, Maui, Hawaii.
    20mm f/4 lens, K 25.

59. Death Valley National Monument, Ca.
    20mm f/4 lens, K 25.

61. McClure Beach, Point Reyes National
    Seashore, Ca.
    80-200mm f/4.5 zoom lens, K 64.

67. Fairlee, Vt.
    20mm f/4 lens, K 25.

68. Bird wing, Bolinas, Ca.
    55mm f/3.5 Micro lens, K 25.

69. Shorebirds, Smith River, Ca.
    80-200mm f/4.5 zoom lens, K 64.

71. Connecticut River near Thetford, Vt.
    80-200mm f/4.5 zoom lens, K 25.

72. Nemo Creek near New Denver,
    British Columbia.
    80-200mm f/4.5 zoom lens, K 25.

73. Slocan Lake, British Columbia.
    20mm f/4 lens, K 25.

74. New Denver Glacier, New Denver,
    British Columbia.
    500mm f/5 Mirror lens, K 25.

77. Icebergs, Glacier Bay, Alaska.
    20mm f/3.5 lens, K II.

78. New Denver, British Columbia.
    20mm f/4 lens, K 25.

79. Reflections, Slocan Lake,
    British Columbia.
    200mm f/4 lens, K II.

81. Bolinas, Ca.
    80-200mm f/4.5 zoom lens, K 64.

83. Mount Cardigan, Vt.
    200mm f/4 lens, K II.